The
Business
of
Ideas

The

Business

of

Ideas

The Highs and Lows of Inventing and
Extracting Revenue from
Intellectual Property

Gregory S Patterson

Artwork by Josh Barrett

authorHOUSE®

AuthorHouse™
1663 Liberty Drive
Bloomington, IN 47403
www.authorhouse.com
Phone: 1-800-839-8640

Published by AuthorHouse   01/22/2013

ISBN: 978-1-4685-8097-6 (sc)
ISBN: 978-1-4685-8096-9 (e)

Library of Congress Control Number: 2012916271

To all of the inventors and tinkerers who have aspirations of turning their ideas into a profitable business.

Acknowledgments

I'd like to thank and acknowledge my father, O. E. "Pat" Patterson, for patiently teaching me how to build things with my hands and J. B. Kelly, who instilled in me the passion to be an inventor.

Contents

The Business of Ideas

1

About the Author

It seems I have always been a tinkerer, at least for as long as I can remember. According to my mother, I show the same fascination for taking apart household items as I have read about in the biographies of other engineers in their youth. Growing up on a farm and having a father who seemed to be able to fix just about any piece of machinery afforded me many opportunities to learn how things worked. As a result, I spent many hours as the tool gopher for my father before it was finally my turn behind the wrench.

The absences of cable TV, Internet, or video games in my youth also gave me plenty of time to dream. Lightning-bolt guns (with aim capability, of course) and hydrostatic-drive, gas-turbine-powered Corvette conversions were among some of the more interesting things that I can remember dreaming about. The ideas seemed as limitless as my imagination.

When it came time to go to college, I debated between trying to become an astronaut and going into engineering. At only four foot nine as a high school senior, I was too short to be accepted as a pilot in the Air Force. So I chose the next best thing: aerospace engineering.

After graduating from North Carolina State University with a BS in aerospace engineering, I was fortunate enough to land a job with the military jet-engine division of Pratt & Whitney. It was there that my tinkering and dreaming culminated in inventing under the guidance of my boss, Jim Kelly. Jim was an active inventor himself and was supportive of my inventive spirit. That support, along with Pratt & Whitney's interest in technology development and intellectual property, proved to be a fertile environment to cultivate my passion for innovation and problem solving.

Many years have passed since those days and my first United States patent: No. 4,959,955 "Method of Operating Gas Turbine Engine with Fan Damage." I currently am named inventor on twenty-nine US patents with multiple foreign patents and others pending. While this is a far cry short of Edison's amazing feat of 1093 patents at the time of his death (ranking him number four worldwide), it does exceed the fifteen-patent threshold for classification as a prolific inventor.

More importantly in the context of this book, I can say with confidence that I have been involved in all aspects of the invention and patenting process in a variety of fields, ranging from jet engines to consumer products.

In 2003, a few colleagues and I started Porticos, Inc., a product-development services company focusing on mechanical product design. We have developed products for many of the Fortune 500 companies, including Dell, Becton-Dickinson, Motorola, Harris Corporation, and Raytheon. It's probably more interesting to the reader that we have also developed some of our own intellectual property. At the time of this writing, the Porticool 2 cooling vest is available on the market as our most recent product. We invented, designed, developed, and then licensed the technology to Shafer Industries under a royalty agreement.

Conversely, we have invented devices that, after proper evaluation, we decided did not promise enough return on our investment to pursue. It is important to know the difference—a topic that I discuss in detail.

What I offer you is a window into the highs and lows of being an inventor and the pitfalls to avoid when trying to generate revenue from your inventions through personal experience and humorous antidotes. Whether you are a tinkerer or a person interested in building a business around your ideas, this book should serve as a very helpful starting reference.

United States Patent [19]

Patterson et al.

[11] Patent Number: 5,072,580

[45] Date of Patent: Dec. 17, 1991

[54] SYSTEM FOR OPERATING GAS TURBINE JET ENGINE WITH FAN DAMAGE

[75] Inventors: Gregory S. Patterson, Stuart; James B. Kelly, Lake Worth, both of Fla.

[73] Assignee: United Technologies Corporation, Hartford, Conn.

[21] Appl. No.: 553,466

[22] Filed: Jul. 17, 1990

Related U.S. Application Data

[62] Division of Ser. No. 316,265, Feb. 27, 1989, Pat. No. 4,959,955.

[51] Int. Cl.⁵ F02K 1/18
[52] U.S. Cl. 60/242; 364/431.02
[58] Field of Search 60/223, 226.1, 233, 60/235, 236, 239, 242, 262; 364/431.02

[56]   References Cited

U.S. PATENT DOCUMENTS

4,139,887	2/1979	Levesque	60/242
4,159,625	7/1979	Kerr	60/236
4,294,069	10/1981	Camp	60/239
4,467,600	8/1984	Peikert	60/204
4,581,880	4/1986	Carpenter et al.	60/242

Primary Examiner—Louis J. Casaregola
Attorney, Agent, or Firm—Edward L. Kochey, Jr.

[57]   ABSTRACT

Normal high load operation automatically varies nozzle area to maintain an optimum engine pressure ratio (EPR). An error signal representing fan damage is established by comparing the actual EPR to the predicted EPR. Compressor stalls are also monitored. In response to these signals a minimum nozzle area is set and modified. Automatic operation to hold EPR and afterburning is inhibited. Further signals representing satisfactory operation may reset the inhibiting action.

11 Claims, 4 Drawing Sheets

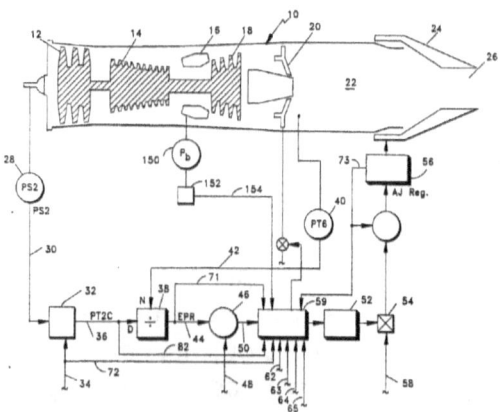

2

Introduction

So, during a recent call with Aunt Sue in Oshkosh, you were sharing with her one of your recent innovative product ideas. Knowing your passion for ideas and inventions, Sue told you the story of her neighbor's grandson Joe, who had a great idea for a new product. After sketching his brainchild on the back of a napkin, he simply got in touch with the right person at the Acme Company, and he'll soon be a "bona fide bazillionaire" because of the royalties. Nothing but piña coladas and palm trees from here on out for lucky Joe.

Now, you're a smart and resourceful inventor, so you think, *Wow, if lucky Joe can strike it rich with* that *idea, I can certainly take my Super-Widget all the way!*

So, all you have to do now is draw up your idea, write down a few notes, contact Acme or one of their competitors, and open a new bank account to stash the fortune.

Well, at the risk of bursting your creative bubble, transforming your great idea into another Aunt Sue story isn't as easy as it may sound. For every success story you hear, there are scores of untold ones in which astute inventors poured their hearts, minds, and financial savings into great ideas to no avail.

Some great ideas will never make it off the drawing board due to existing patents or products, lack of interest, or aversion to risk. Others will make it to market only to fail financially due to marketing, timing, or legal issues. Regardless, the process of bringing a good idea to reality can be long and arduous, and it's not recommended for the faint of heart.

The hook-and-loop fastening system more commonly known as Velcro is one well-known example of a good idea that was successfully navigated to the market. Velcro, a combination of two French words—*velour* and *crochet*—was patented by George de Mestral in 1955.

In a process known today as biomimicry (the science that examines nature in order to create models or processes that imitate life), the kernel for Mestral's idea came during a walk with his dog. He was intrigued by a plant's seed sacs that clung to his dog's fur. Inspection under a microscope revealed small hooks that enabled the seed sacs to cling to his dog's fur.

Mestral also noted that the hooks clung just as viciously to the tiny loops in the fabric of his clothing, so if he could design a similar two-sided fastener system, it would rival the zipper in its ability to fasten.

It took nearly eight years of research and trial and error before he was able to develop a mechanized process for replicating the small hooks that mimic the seed sac that inspired his idea.

Mestral borrowed money and formed Velcro Industries to manufacture his invention. Initial sales were disappointing as the product was met with resistance and even laughter. However, the perseverance paid off when NASA started using Velcro in its spacesuits. Soon Velcro started showing up in sports apparel and children's clothing, and sales reached sixty million yards per year. Mestral became a multimillionaire because of his invention and was inducted into the National Inventors Hall of Fame in 1999.

Today Velcro is a household name, but it wasn't an automatic success. Its success required perseverance, a little luck, an unwavering passion, and faith in the idea. But what are the odds of success?

As most inventors know, applying for and being awarded a utility patent for an invention—otherwise known as intellectual property—is typically a prerequisite for extracting value from it. Without this level of protection, anyone who learns of your invention can produce it and sell it as his or her own, without any compensation to you. According to statistics on intellectual property generated by Bell Labs, for every ten thousand ideas generated with the intention of patenting, one thousand make it to the point of becoming disclosures, or patent applications. Of those, ten generate some value. Just in case you think you really have a revolutionary idea, of those original ten thousand ideas, one will result in a change in the industry, as Velcro did. What this boils down to is that for every thousand ideas generated, one ends up returning value to the inventor. These statistics are consistent with research presented in other publications, which range in estimates from one in five hundred[1] to one in five thousand ideas.[2] If you look at the US Patent and Trademark Office website (www.uspto.gov), you get a further indication on how high the bar is to generate and gain intellectual property rights for an idea. Based on the US Patent Statistics Chart, published by the USPTO, there were 535,188 patent applications submitted in the United States in 2011. According to the latest census, there were roughly 311,800,000 people in the United States at that time. Statistically speaking, only one person in 583 has an idea that reaches the point of patent application. Because committed inventors don't typically stop with one patent application (according to a recent statistic on Wikipedia, the average is three per inventor), even this estimation is optimistic.

A quote from Richard Maulsby, director of the Office of Public Affairs at the US Patent and Trademark Office, seems to summarize this chapter: "In truth, odds are stacked astronomically against the inventor, and no marketing outfit can change them."

---

[1]   Karen E. Klein, "Avoiding the Inventor's Lament," *Businessweek*, November 10, 2005.
[2]   Bevolyn Williams-Harold, "You've got it made!" *Black Enterprise*, June 1, 1999.

Now you may be wondering, *What's the purpose of this book?* Based on what you've read so far, it sounds like the odds of success are long and the work is hard. *Why would I want to be an inventor?*

The purpose of this book is to make you fully aware of the costs and processes associated with patenting an idea. And if you're interested in starting or building a business around an idea, I want to give you the tools and experience to help determine if the investment will be worth the risk.

It's not my intention to discourage you from pursuing your inventive creativity. Rather, I want to protect you from being scammed by the seemingly endless number of get-rich-quick con artists that wait around every corner. This book will help you determine what level of risk you're comfortable with taking and what commitment to the invention process you're willing to make.

The answer to the second question—Why would I want to be an inventor?"—is more philosophical. If you have an inventive spirit, you just can't help it. And why should you? The fact is, it's fun to invent new products. It's exciting when you have a new challenge that you don't immediately know the answer to. It's rewarding when, after months of failures, your prototype begins functioning as you planned. So don't shy away from the ideas that continually come to your mind. Embrace them and enjoy the ride.

US007064655B2

(12) United States Patent
Murray et al.

(10) Patent No.: **US 7,064,655 B2**
(45) Date of Patent: **Jun. 20, 2006**

(54) **VARIABLE-ECCENTRICITY TACTILE GENERATOR**

(75) Inventors: **Matthew J. Murray**, Raleigh, NC (US); **Michael Townsend**, Durham, NC (US); **Chris Eaton**, Cary, NC (US); **Gregory S. Patterson**, Morrisville, NC (US)

(73) Assignee: **Sony Ericsson Mobile Communications AB** (SE)

(*) Notice: Subject to any disclaimer, the term of this patent is extended or adjusted under 35 U.S.C. 154(b) by 179 days.

(21) Appl. No.: **10/827,044**

(22) Filed: **Apr. 19, 2004**

(65) **Prior Publication Data**

US 2005/0140503 A1 Jun. 30, 2005

Related U.S. Application Data

(60) Provisional application No. 60/533,644, filed on Dec. 31, 2003.

(51) Int. Cl.
H04B 3/36 (2006.01)
(52) U.S. Cl. **340/407.1**; 340/679; 340/683; 340/686.3
(58) Field of Classification Search 340/679, 340/683, 686.3, 407.1
See application file for complete search history.

(56) **References Cited**

U.S. PATENT DOCUMENTS

3,920,222 A *	11/1975	Bunder	366/114
4,034,614 A	7/1977	Fers et al.	
6,323,757 B1	11/2001	Nagni	
6,603,622 B1 *	2/2004	Shabsian et al	345/156
6,711,258 B1	3/2004	Sung	

FOREIGN PATENT DOCUMENTS

DE	18 04 955	5/1969
EP	0 667 672	8/1995
WO	WO 91/20136	12/1991

OTHER PUBLICATIONS

PCT International Search Report; International Application No. PCT/US2004/020409; mailed Nov. 30, 2004.

* cited by examiner

Primary Examiner—Daryl C. Pope
(74) *Attorney, Agent, or Firm*—Coats & Bennett, P.L.L.C.

(57) **ABSTRACT**

A tactile generator comprises an eccentric mass that imparts a vibration as it rotates about a rotational axis. The mass is radially movable with respect to the rotational axis such that the distance between the mass and the axis is variable. Varying the distance of the mass from the axis varies the amount of vibration generated when the mass is rotated. The amount of vibration may be controlled responsive to a detected level of ambient noise.

45 Claims, 8 Drawing Sheets

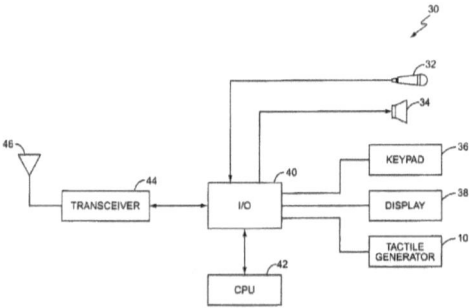

3

Risk Versus Reward

It has often been said that there are no rewards without risks. What people fail to consider when evaluating ideas for development is how much risk they are capable of taking—and not strictly monetarily. Risks include development risks of time and technology as well as liability risks that will be attached to the final product. The more risk you are willing or able to take, the higher the return you may expect. So, what are some of the risks to consider?

The most obvious risk factor is cost. How much capital or access to capital do you have, and what level of debt are you comfortable with? I equate this to bidding on eBay. It's better to go into the auction with a set limit that you're willing to spend. Otherwise, you can find yourself in a bidding war that makes the final sale price higher than the item's retail value.

Once you've established your line in the sand, you can then establish how you are going to proceed. Are you able to go it alone, or do you need additional investment? This will help you determine whether you can expect to take this idea into production yourself or focus on prototyping it with the hopes of licensing the technology to a company with deeper pockets.

In my opinion, the second most important risk factor is the level of liability the product will be exposed to. This affects not only your costs (liability insurance for a safety product can be very expensive), but also may affect your family's security. Ask yourself, *What is the effect if the product fails to perform?* Remember that failures do not need to be purely the result of design or manufacturing issues. There are plenty of examples of successful litigation in which the user's stupidity was the root cause. Is someone's life at risk if the product fails to perform? If the answer is yes, prepare financially and mentally to ward off the inevitable lawsuit.

Don't try to convince yourself that a lawsuit won't happen. If you aren't comfortable with the risk, stay away from manufacturing the product yourself and focus on licensing the technology. Granted, even that doesn't fully absolve you of implication in a lawsuit. But it does add layers of shielding between you and the plaintiff.

A third risk factor is associated with investing your time and energy in developing the idea. How much time do you need to spend to get the required return on your investment? This is especially important to explore if you have several ideas worthy of development or if your primary professional income is derived from something other than inventing. Can you afford the risk of going down the rabbit hole for six months or a year to champion the idea instead of supporting your other obligations?

Once you have read this book, you will have a better understanding of what development of an idea entails and what the potential rewards can be. Use that understanding to determine if the risk of applying your time to this idea is economically justifiable.

I'll add one other comment on the topic of your time investment. You need to consider your personal obligations as well as your fiscal obligations. If this is a second job or hobby, how will your spouse react to the additional time out in the shop? Do you have children or other family commitments that you need to consider? While the financial aspects and risks of building a business usually are weighted heavily in the beginning of any venture, I suspect that personal turmoil is often a major contributing factor in a venture's downfall.

Once you've evaluated your capacity for risk in these areas, it will be easier for you to determine what level of involvement you can make in developing your idea. It will also help you to plan for that development. Should you try to license the technology, or will you take the idea into production and become your own sales and distribution channel?

United States Patent [19]

Patterson

[11] Patent Number:	**5,790,661**
[45] Date of Patent:	**Aug. 4, 1998**

[54] **MOUNT PLATE FOR THE CRADLE OF A TELEPHONE**

[75] Inventor: **Gregory S. Patterson**. Morrisville. N.C.

[73] Assignee: **Ericsson Inc.**. Research Triangle Park. N.C.

[21] Appl. No.: **715,474**

[22] Filed: **Sep. 18, 1996**

[51] **Int. Cl.⁶** **H04M 1/00**
[52] **U.S. Cl.** **379/446**; 379/455
[58] **Field of Search** .... 379/426. 435.
379/436. 455. 454. 446; 248/221.12. 221.14.
222.41. 223.41. 224.8; 455/90. 347. 569

[56] **References Cited**

U.S. PATENT DOCUMENTS

2,107,885	2/1938	Caggiano	248/223.41
4,226,394	10/1980	Einhorn	248/223.41

4,944,416   7/1990 Peterson etal 248/223.41

Primary Examiner—Jack Chiang
Attorney, Agent, or Firm—Nixon & Vanderhye

[57] **ABSTRACT**

A mount plate for the cradle of a telephone has a forward and upwardly inclined projecting boss with a concave surface through which a traverse slot is provided. An enlarged access opening is provided in the traverse slot for receiving a nut loosely secured on a bolt passing through the cradle. By sliding the nut and bolt from the access opening along the slot, a cam surface of the traverse slot automatically rotates the nut into proper orientation to hold it between constraining rails along the underside of the slot enabling tightening of the bolt relative to the nut. The access opening is sized and configured such that the nut can be received through the opening. Once rotated into the tightening position, the nut can also be tightened in underlying relation to the opening, affording a substantial range of movement of the cradle along the traverse slot.

15 Claims, 3 Drawing Sheets

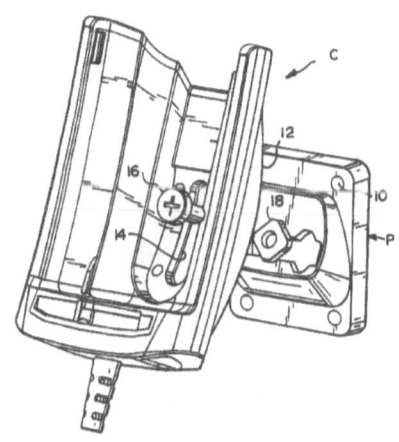

4

By the Numbers: Cost

Successful ideas are backed up by the numbers. Everyone's idea is the *greatest* idea to him or her, but if the return on investment doesn't offer an attractive return, it's probably not worth going forward. What is an attractive Return on Investment (ROI)? There isn't a firm number, because it depends on the circumstances, but a good goal is 10:1. For every one dollar you invest, you want to get a net return of ten dollars.

I've found that the best way to determine the ROI is by creating a spreadsheet that organizes all investments and revenue. Once you have these two categories defined, the ROI is a simple calculation (revenue / investment). Unfortunately, determining the investments (expenses) and revenue is not a straightforward process. There are assumptions you have to make. The goal is to make your assumptions as accurate as possible.

It's worth noting that, regardless of whether you plan to license the technology or manufacture and sell the product yourself, you need to calculate the ROI from the perspective of manufacturing and selling the product. That's because you need some of those numbers to help determine the potential royalty and also because it will help you in your negotiations with the licensee. The more prepared you are, the better your chances of interesting a buyer and inking a good deal.

Let's consider the various details of a spreadsheet and how to improve the accuracy of your assumptions, starting with the expense side of the sheet:

1. Material costs: The best approach is to create a complete list of all parts that constitute the product. Include everything from major components to the smallest parts, such as screws, tapes, or labels. The accuracy of your Build of Materials (BOM) is dependent on how well your concept is defined. When in doubt, err to the conservative side. If you aren't sure how it is going to be held together, plan on screws instead of snaps, etc.

Once you have the list, enter cost estimates for these parts. This requires that you make more assumptions. Part costs are a factor of manufacturing material (plastic, metal, wood, etc.) manufacturing processes (injection molding, progressive die, machined, etc.), and manufacturing volume. Typically, the more you make of something the less the part will cost. This is the result of being able to spread setup and related tooling costs (fixed costs) over a larger number of parts, which reduces the cost per part.

Next, determine what your quantity will be. Refer to the marketing research suggestions covered in chapter 10 to help you determine the size of the market for your product. Consider how much of that market you expect to capture.

Start small. It will take time to wrestle much of the market from the current competition. You should not be surprised to gain only 5 percent market share in the first full year, with growth to 20 percent in year five.

Also make an estimate of the part cost (and fixed costs such as tooling, etc.). If you work closely with the material and manufacturing processes needed to build your product, you might be comfortable making cost estimates based on your experience. If not, don't be afraid to contact manufacturing sources and get preliminary quotes. Again, the accuracy of the quote will be subject to the completeness of the design, so keep that in mind.

Finally, consider any assembly and subassembly costs. This will be related to the time it takes to do the assembly and the hourly rate. You will need to estimate what those times and rates will be. If you've built a prototype, just time the various assembly activities. Regarding the rate, consider if the product will be made domestically or overseas, and enter a value based on rates in those fields.

Now add fifteen to twenty cents per assembly for shipping, and multiply the entire part cost by 20 percent to take into account unknowns, manufacturing profits, and so on. That will give you the cost per part.

ROI goals are usually based on a period of time (typically three to five years), so to get the total investment for materials, multiply the cost per part by the volumes expected over the period, and add the fixed costs (like tooling, etc.). This will be your total investment in material over the period.

2. Resource costs: This category takes into account the costs to design, develop, and industrialize the concept. If you are in the business of product design, you're well

positioned to estimate this cost. If not, you will probably face a combination of work you can do versus work you will end up outsourcing to a consultant or design firm.

As you might imagine, the amount of effort required is directly related to the complexity of the design and the manufacturing processes involved. As a rule of thumb, most products take between six and eighteen months to design and bring into production. Design firms typically charge between 100 and 150 dollars per engineering hour. The number of engineers ranges from one engineer for simple products to a team of ten, hundreds, or thousands in extreme cases, such as automotive or aircraft design.

Assuming you aren't competing directly with Ford or Pratt&Whitney, you'll likely find yourself needing between one and five engineers. This can range from a hundred thousand to two million dollars. You need to determine where in this range you expect to be.

3. Business-related costs: These costs include insurance, office space, utilities, marketing, and so on. While you might be tempted to assume that these costs will be negligible, they can add up quickly. Product liability insurance can be very expensive, particularly if the failure mode (regardless of the cause) can result in bodily injury. For example, one simple

product we developed and manufactured for the pet industry required liability insurance with a ten-thousand-dollar annual premium.

Marketing is another area that can quickly add up. Advertisement in publications, exhibiting at trade shows, and radio, TV, or Internet ads are all valid marketing options. A one-time, half-page add in a popular magazine can easily cost 1,500 to 3,000 dollars. TV ads can run from 20,000 to one million and beyond if you're hoping for the Super Bowl crowd. Most industry trade shows cost three thousand dollars for a ten-by-ten booth, and you need to add the cost of the display and other items. You will most likely require some combination of these options, easily incurring twenty thousand to one hundred thousand dollars' worth of expense for even a simple product in a short period.

4. Patent and legal costs: Account for the cost to patent your idea and legal costs related to licensing the idea if you decide to go that route. You can refer to the USPTO website for the complete and up-to-date menu of services and related fees. Those fees alone can range from 2,400 to $3,000 dollars to file a utility patent, depending on whether you are doing a search or not. Plus, there are extension fees (150 to 2,690 dollars), appeals fees (400 to 1,240), petition fees (130 to 1,860), Patent Cooperation Treaty (PCT) fees if you want to have the option to file your patent in a foreign country (380 to 2,500), and numerous other fees that you may or may not need to consider.

    Do not confuse the PCT fee with the cost to file for a patent in a foreign country. It is intended only to hold your invention date and give you a one-year grace period before you need to file in the foreign country of your choice. Foreign filings are very expensive; they can easily be 30,000 dollars, depending on the country you wish to file for patent protection in.

    If you have a patent attorney to draft the patent, you need to figure on 250 dollars per hour for his or her services. As a benchmark, the least expensive patent I ever submitted for a simple mechanical hinge mechanism still cost just over six thousand dollars in patent attorney fees. The costs can add up quickly, depending on the complexity.

Assuming you are awarded a patent, you'll have maintenance fees. These are due at 3.5 years (1,130 dollars), 7.5 years (2,850) and 11.5 years (4,730). Failure to pay these maintenance fees will result in your patent expiring and open the door for anyone to manufacture and sell a product using your technology.

When I worked in one large corporation, I was told that they budget one hundred thousand dollars per patent for attorney and filing fees. That might be extreme for a small inventor, but, assuming that you write the patent without an attorney, everything is accepted with no rejections that require appeals, and you maintain the patent for its full life, you will need to consider in your investment about a 12,000-dollar minimum just in USPTO fees.

Similarly, if you are planning to license the idea or even form your own company, consider what legal fees you will need to pay. Again, at 250 dollars per hour, it doesn't take long to rack up substantial expenses. I would consider ten to twenty hours minimum for an attorney to draft and/or review a licensing agreement for you.

This chapter can often be very discouraging for the first-time inventor or budding entrepreneur. But that's not my intent. It is the unfiltered truth that you don't get from infomercials trying to sell you a packet on patenting your idea. I prefer to have all of the information as I go into my investment, rather than find out halfway down the road, and I suspect you do to. Information is power, and with it you can make the best decision regarding the level of risk you're comfortable with taking.

(12) **United States Patent**
Patterson

(10) Patent No.: **US 6,362,791 B1**
(45) Date of Patent: **Mar. 26, 2002**

(54) **PORTABLE COMMUNICATION DEVICE HOLDER AND ANTENNA**

(75) Inventor: **Gregory Scott Patterson**, Morrisville, NC (US)

(73) Assignee: **Ericsson Inc.**, Research Triangle Park, NC (US)

(*) Notice: Subject to any disclaimer, the term of this patent is extended or adjusted under 35 U.S.C. 154(b) by 0 days.

(21) Appl. No.: **09/521,345**

(22) Filed: **Mar. 9, 2000**

(51) Int. Cl.[7] H01Q 1/24
(52) U.S. Cl. **343/702**; 343/878; 343/880; 455/575
(58) Field of Search 343/702, 712, 343/713, 718, 878, 880, 883, 882; 455/348, 351, 575, 90, 345, 346, 347, 349; 248/537, 683; H01Q 1/24, 1/32

(56) **References Cited**

U.S. PATENT DOCUMENTS

5,281,970 A * 1/1994 Blaese 343/878

5,640,316 A	7/1997	Prudhomme et al 455/345
5,861,857 A	1/1999	Kozak 343/711
5,945,956 A	8/1999	Izawa et al. 343/713

* cited by examiner

Primary Examiner—Michael C. Wimer
(74) Attorney, Agent, or Firm—Myers Bigel Sibley & Sajovec

(57) **ABSTRACT**

An antenna designed integral to a windshield holder for a portable communications device is provided. The antenna can be an integral part of the windshield holder or an attachment to it. The windshield holder attaches to the windshield of a vehicle by a securing mount to which is attached an extension. The extension has attached, at a location different from the securing mount, a device mount for a portable communications device. The securing mount, device mount, and extension may all be adjustable for mounting in varying positions and locations. The windshield holder is easily attached and removed from the windshield improving both transportability and security. The antenna connects to the phone by a connector or interface at the phone mount, either automatically, when the portable communications device is inserted in the device mount, or by a separate operation.

8 Claims, 4 Drawing Sheets

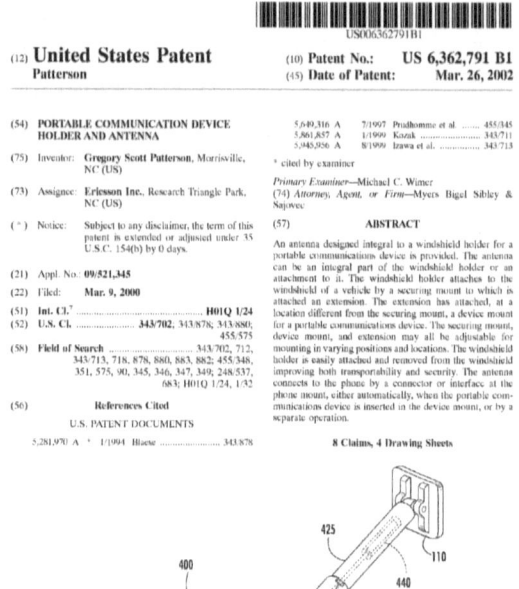

5

By the Numbers: Revenue

Now that we understand some of the cost associated with developing a product, let's consider the revenue side of the equation. In the last chapter, you already assumed what your sales volumes will be. The next step is to estimate how much the product will sell for.

The first approach is to calculate what the sale price will be "bottoms up"—starting with the manufacturing price and ending with the retail price. Take the BOM part costs you developed earlier and multiply by two. This will give you what the preferred distributor price would be. For example, if you calculated the manufacturing cost at one dollar, then you would sell to a distributor for two, netting you one. Note that this isn't necessarily one dollar in profit; you still have many other expenses, as we've discussed. It is simply a one-dollar gain over the cost to manufacture the product. Remember the pet product that required ten thousand dollars for liability insurance? We would have to sell over ten thousand units per year just to cover that one line item if our net return on sales is only one dollar.

Now take the distributor cost (two dollars in this example) and multiply by two again. This will give you the wholesale price (four dollars in this example). This is the price a store would pay to buy the product and put it on its shelves. Now multiply the wholesale price by two (eight dollars) to get the suggested retail price. This is the price the end consumer would pay. Granted, these factors are budgetary only. The product might sell direct (no distributor markup) to a retail chain. Similarly, the 2X factor can range to 1.3 or lower, depending on what arrangement you negotiate with the distributor or retail chain along with other factors. But, in general, a 2X factor is a good starting point.

This brings us to yet another assumption. What will the market bear? The easiest way to determine if your product sale price is something consumers will accept is to look at the actual retail prices of competitive products. People might be willing to pay more for higher quality or more innovative features, but probably less than you would like to imagine, but you are going to need to stay competitive with your pricing to entice the buyer.

Look at our example: how does the eight-dollar product stack up with the competing products? Be honest in your assessment. If they are in close competition, you can feel more comfortable that your revenue and sales volume estimates are achievable. If you aren't sure, you might want to invest in the aid of a marketing company to do some price elasticity studies. But bear this in mind: there is no guarantee of success.

We are now ready to calculate our revenue. Simply multiply the sales volumes by the distributor sale price. This will give you the revenue. If you want to be more accurate, consider what percentage you plan to sell to distributors—retail or direct—and factor those additional revenues into your equation. Be careful not to use this practice to make a poor return marginal. You will only be fooling yourself. You can now calculate ROI. How does it compare to your 10:1 goal?

If your plan is to license the technology, do a few more calculations. Starting with the investment side of the equation, eliminate the material expenses except for costs you do expect to incur, such as prototype costs. Evaluate resource and business expenses similarly.

The next assumption is to determine how much in these two categories you will need. At a minimum, you will need to devote some time and resources to developing the idea to the point that potential investors will be able to appreciate the concept. But marketing costs will probably diminish greatly, since the company you re licensing the technology to would most likely already have advertisement and sales channels.

Likewise, consider changes to the revenue side of the equation. Primarily, your revenue will be based on royalty from the sale of the product. Royalty agreements are varied and highly dependent on negotiations, market potential, and other factors. A typical agreement would be based on some percentage of the revenue generated from the sale of the product. Basically, we're talking about the distributor sale price times sales volume times some percentage for royalty. Assume a royalty percentage of 10 to 20 percent in your calculations. This will give you what your revenue from royalties could be.

Note that it's common for the licensor to get some money up front as a good-faith payment to show the licensor that the licensee will have incentive to go forward with the technology and take it into production. I recommend that you *not* consider that in your revenue calculations. The reason is twofold. First, upfront payments are not guaranteed. Second, they are often considered advancements on the royalty. Effectively, they are diluted when sales volumes start to reach the targets you've already accounted for in the royalty payments.

That's it. You are now capable of calculating the ROI from the licensing perspective. How does this ROI look to you? One thing you should notice is that the ROI is substantially less than the ROI from a manufacturing and sales perspective, which is consistent with the risk-versus-reward philosophy we discussed previously.

We've focused on a lot of numbers and assumptions in this chapter. Hopefully, you haven't been scared off by the process or level of effort required.

Don't overlook these important steps. While many inventors are more interested in the benefits to humankind that their technology can provide, all businesses must generate revenue. At the risk of stating the obvious, revenue must equal or preferably exceed expenses. Otherwise, you won't be in business long.

So take your time and do the proper research to make sure your idea will yield the ROI you need to justify the risk before you invest too much of your time and money.

United States Patent [19]

Patterson et al.

[11] **Patent Number:** **5,867,877**

[45] **Date of Patent:** **Feb. 9, 1999**

[54] **SELF-RELEASING COUPLER**

[75] Inventors: **Gregory S. Patterson**, Morrisville, N.C.; **Mark Welsh**, West Palm Beach, Fla.

[73] Assignee: **Turtle Snaps, Inc.**, Palm Beach Gardens, Fla.

[21] Appl. No.: **911,665**

[22] Filed: **Aug. 15, 1997**

[51] Int. Cl.⁶ **A44B 21/00**
[52] U.S. Cl. **24/598.5**; 24/517; 24/600.7; 24/602
[58] Field of Search .... 24/598.5, 602, 24/599.4, 599.5, 599.7, 600.2, 601.5, 115 F

[56] **References Cited**

U.S. PATENT DOCUMENTS

1,262,974	4/1918	Pearen	24/598.5
1,299,821	4/1919	Carpmill et al.	24/598.5
1,684,322	9/1928	Iljen	24/598.5
3,235,928	2/1966	Clark	24/517
3,540,089	11/1970	Franklin	24/602
3,952,382	4/1976	Vinge	24/600.7
4,315,424	2/1982	Jarman et al.	24/525
4,733,625	3/1988	Allen	24/602
5,430,914	7/1995	Patterson et al.	24/598.5
5,600,782	3/1997	Patterson et al.	24/598.5

Primary Examiner—Victor N. Sakran
Attorney, Agent, or Firm—Rhodes, Coats & Bennett, L.L.P.

[57] **ABSTRACT**

A self-releasing or break-away coupler that releases in response to experiencing a predetermined load. The self-releasing coupler includes a pair of jaws that form a fastener. Surrounding the jaws is a sleeve housing that deforms in response to the predetermined load when applied to the jaws. That is, as the housing deforms, the jaws are allowed to open so as to release a fastener or connector secured within the jaws.

16 Claims, 5 Drawing Sheets

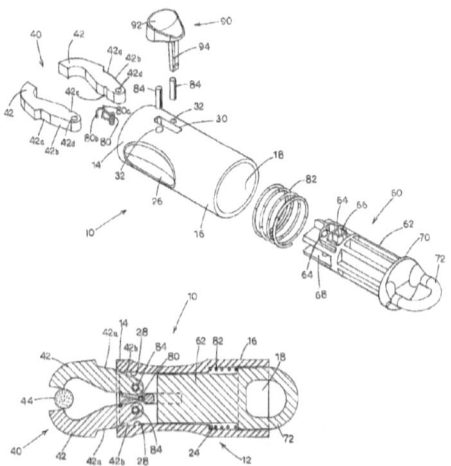

6

Single-Product Myth

In the introduction, I talked about some of the challenges and odds associated with filing, receiving, and profiting from your ideas. In this chapter, I'll explore another common misconception that many people have, which I call the "single-product myth." You know, the little voice deep down that says, "If I could just come up with that one great idea, I'd be walking on easy street."

The truth is, it takes more than a single idea or product to build a business. First are the unfavorable odds you have to consider. I'm not going down that path again here, since we've already discussed it in detail, but the chance that your idea will produce a monetary return is fairly low. To be successful, you need to have a portfolio of ideas or products to work with. I compare this to the general disclaimer your investment manager would give you on the importance of diversification. The more ideas you have, the larger your intellectual property portfolio can be, and the greater your base will be for generating a return on your investment.

I suspect that you may be twitching in your seat. Surely many entrepreneurs have started a company on the premise of a single idea and reaped the rewards, right? What about Bill Gates at Microsoft or Steve Jobs at Apple? Those guys seem to have a pretty hefty bankroll.

I admit it is not impossible, and I suspect you have good stories to tell, but give me a chance to defend my position.

Maybe it's just semantics, but I would argue that Bill Gates started with a *vision* rather than with a *product idea*. There is a difference. Under his vision and leadership, the engineers at Microsoft were able to develop a large portfolio and wide range of products over time. A simple search on the US Patent and Trademark Organization site shows a large number of patents assigned to Microsoft. A close look inside the nearest computer or software store for products Microsoft is involved with will probably astound you. Gates was creative, had a vision, and surrounded himself with other creative people to develop innovative products in support of his vision. He had a knack for business, and he was a little lucky to boot. Any way you look at it, that's a good combination.

Look at the flip side of that example: I know a couple of engineers that had a pretty good idea for a product to address a real problem in the equine marketplace. They used their engineering skills and developed a solution with good results. They were successful in getting a couple of patents on the product and put together a solid business case. With help from a few private investors, they were even able to launch into production. Although the product was well received and garnered positive reviews, it barely covered the cost of manufacturing, even after eight years.

Of course, manufacturing costs are only one of the expenses that a company faces, as we have discussed. The limited market for the company's sole product combined with the sales margin that the market would bear prevented the company from generating enough revenue to offset those other expenses. Ultimately, the company was forced to sell the patents and manufacturing equipment to another company at no profit.

This was not what you would call a financial success story by any measure. I can say this comfortably, since I was one of the engineers in this story. That's why I wanted to write this book: to prevent others from having the experience I had as a young, novice inventor / entrepreneur.

So, why did Microsoft succeed where the equine product company failed? You could argue (and I think that you'd be right) that the kernel of what became Microsoft was stronger by comparison because of a number of factors, many of which I address in this book. However, other factors aside, I contend that the equine product company may have been successful if it had expanded its product offering.

Why do I make this contention? Because the company that bought the patent and manufacturing equipment is still producing that product today. The product is called the Turtle Snap, and it's just one of the many products offered by Davis Manufacturing for the equine market. This innovative product addresses a need in the equine market by providing a safer means of securing a horse in a trailer or stable area.

Davis Manufacturing uses the same materials, supplier base, and cost structure that we used, but its larger product portfolio allows for two substantial advantages. First, it can distribute overhead expenses over a larger product base. Second, it opens opportunities to large retailers. These retailers have sourcing policies that discourage adding smaller companies to the approved supplier list. Rather, they prefer to negotiate with larger distributors or suppliers that can offer savings over a broad product offering. Larger retail outlets generate a larger market for the Turtle Snap, ultimately resulting in higher sales. How? If you're shopping at Walmart for necessities, you're apt to add items to your cart that you hadn't planned to purchase. The Turtle Snap benefits from such unplanned buys.

Still not convinced? Go to any store or mall or flea market, and what do you see? A store or booth with just one item? No! The retailers might focus on a particular market, but they have a multitude of products on the shelves. For example, a candle shop has a variety of candles, plus various knick-knacks and accessories. This is the same whether you are in retail or in developing products. The sooner you come to that realization, the better.

So, what should you learn from this? That you face an insurmountable task, so you should just give up and sit on the couch in front of the TV? Absolutely not! Just realize that if innovation is a cornerstone on which you are going to build a business, it can't be a part-time endeavor. You have to look continually and actively for problems—or opportunities as the self-help books say. You have to develop innovative solutions to those problems, and you have to build your business portfolio while remaining aligned with the overall vision of the company.

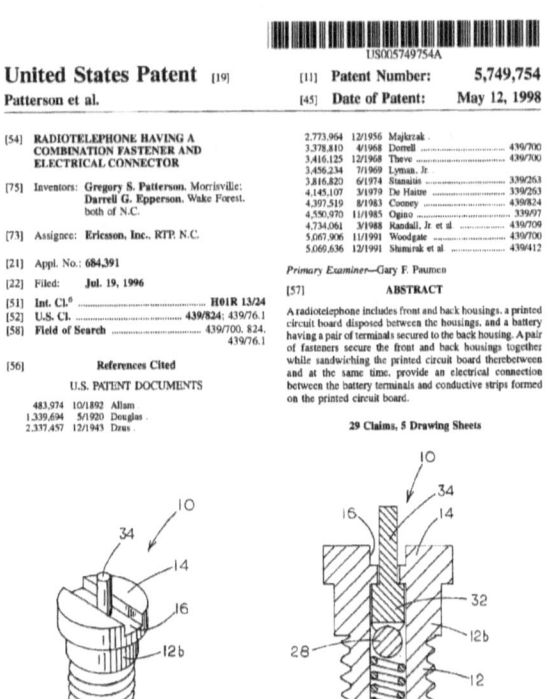

US005749754A

United States Patent [19]

Patterson et al.

[11] Patent Number: **5,749,754**

[45] Date of Patent: May 12, 1998

[54] **RADIOTELEPHONE HAVING A COMBINATION FASTENER AND ELECTRICAL CONNECTOR**

[75] Inventors: **Gregory S. Patterson**, Morrisville; **Darrell G. Epperson**, Wake Forest, both of N.C.

[73] Assignee: **Ericsson, Inc.**, RTP, N.C.

[21] Appl. No.: **684,391**

[22] Filed: **Jul. 19, 1996**

[51] **Int. Cl.⁶** **H01R 13/24**
[52] **U.S. Cl.** **439/824**; 439/76.1
[58] **Field of Search** 439/700, 824, 439/76.1

[56] **References Cited**

U.S. PATENT DOCUMENTS

483,974	10/1892	Allum .
1,339,694	5/1920	Douglas .
2,337,457	12/1943	Dzus .
2,773,964	12/1956	Majkrzak .
3,378,810	4/1968	Dorrell 439/700
3,416,125	12/1968	Theve 439/700
3,456,234	7/1969	Lyman, Jr.
3,816,820	6/1974	Stanalis 339/263
4,145,107	3/1979	De Haitre 339/263
4,397,519	8/1983	Cooney 439/824
4,550,970	11/1985	Ogino 339/97
4,734,061	3/1988	Randall, Jr. et al. 439/709
5,067,906	11/1991	Woodgate 439/700
5,069,636	12/1991	Shumrak et al. 439/412

*Primary Examiner—*Gary F. Paumen

[57] **ABSTRACT**

A radiotelephone includes front and back housings, a printed circuit board disposed between the housings, and a battery having a pair of terminals secured to the back housing. A pair of fasteners secure the front and back housings together while sandwiching the printed circuit board therebetween and at the same time, provide an electrical connection between the battery terminals and conductive strips formed on the printed circuit board.

29 Claims, 5 Drawing Sheets

7

Passion

Passion. It's a word we often use, though we usually hear it used in the context of romance. Webster's defines passion as "intense, driving, or overmastering feeling or conviction, a strong liking or desire for or devotion to some activity, object, or concept." What's does this have to do with the *inventing*? More than you might think.

I would define passion in inventing as an insatiable desire to develop new and novel ways of solving problems or expanding technology. Typically, the answers aren't easily found, and thought, research, and experimentation are required to prove the solutions. Inventors' passion drives them to put in the effort that most others would shy away from. It is akin to taking the road less traveled. I'm comfortable saying that passion for innovation is the cornerstone on which a successful inventor builds his or her portfolio.

As you've learned thus far, developing and driving an idea from concept to the market isn't for the faint of heart. Innovation has to be a passion, and the kernel of an idea must excite the inventor, or it won't stand the rigors of development.

Let's take a little quiz to see if you have the passion necessary to weather the storm. Feel free to get your pen or pencil out and circle the answers that best represent how an inventor would respond to the different scenarios.

1) When you face a simple task that your standard assortment of tools just isn't cut out to handle, what do you do?

a) Fabricate a special tool to get the job done, even though the fabrication process will take longer than doing the job in the first place.

b) Do a time-value study comparing your salary to the cost of outsourcing, and decide to hire someone to come in and do the job for you.

c) Put the task at the bottom of your "honey do" list with the hope that you will never get that far down the list?

2. When you're pushing the cart and following your significant other around the aisles of your local Walmart, what do you do?

a) Mentally design a new five-quart motor oil container that would also serve as the drain pan for capturing and recycling the old oil.

b) Daydream about your busy afternoon lying on the couch and watching the Eagles lose yet another playoff game.

c) Shake your head, amazed at the fact that no matter what you came in to get, you always leave with a cartload of stuff you didn't need.

3) When you're standing at the magazine rack in your local bookstore, what do you find yourself reading?

a) The history of the alarm siren in the latest *Invention and Technology* magazine.

b) The Red Hot Chili Peppers interview in *Rolling Stone*.

c) *Oprah* magazine or the swimsuit edition of *Sports Illustrated*.

4) When it's time to clean the leaves out of the gutters on your house, what do you do?

a) Go to your local hardware store, buy some PVC pipe, some flexible hose, and some duct tape, and then create an attachment for your leaf blower so you can walk along the ground while blowing the leaves out of your gutter.

b) Get a ladder and yo-yo your way around the house, systematically cleaning the leaves out three feet at a time.

c) Tell your kids to climb out the second-story window onto the roof and go clean out the gutters.

Okay, put your pencil or pen down. Although I won't profess that this is a scientific questionnaire, it's probably obvious that we're looking for the answer A in all of these questions as symptomatic of someone who has a passion for innovation (except for question three, which may have two correct answers for men). While it may not always be the best or most practical answer, a true inventor is always willing to take twice the effort just to develop an idea.

What if you didn't answer A for all the questions, but you are undaunted in your resolve to be an inventor. *Can't I just make it a job?* you ask yourself. After all, you probably spend the greater part of your day doing things you don't like. What's wrong with adding one more? I wish you all the best, but it's been my experience that this approach doesn't work.

During my career in management, I got to test this out. I had a team of smart, hard-working folks. Though we worked in a technical environment, everyone agreed that sometimes we lacked the opportunity to be innovative; the pressures of product development don't usually afford the time to tinker with unproven ideas. So I decided that I would reward some of the engineers in the team who were just finishing a hard tour of duty on the project front by allowing them to focus strictly on innovating a new widget. The goal was to develop some new concepts and do some rough order feasibility investigations to see if the concepts could be viable.

To my surprise, it quickly became apparent that the reward was anything but. They became distracted by all sorts of mundane tasks—often seeking those tasks out. Without the whip of project goals and an orderly task list and without the passion to innovate around the parameters of a kernel, the results were lack luster. I suspect it was only because they were dedicated engineers who felt a responsibility to produce something that the investigation yielded any results at all.

That exercise was a stark reminder that what might be considered fun or challenging to one person isn't necessarily that way for another, and vice versa.

So, what's the purpose of this story? Innovation is not a simple check-the-box process. Even for those few boxes that are there, the goal isn't to put the check in the box; the box is intended to spawn ideas and provide rough guidance. Just making it your job (or someone else's) will rarely result in a valuable invention.

Don't be disheartened if your personal reflection is leading you to understand that perhaps you're not an inventor. Building a business based on ideas takes unique skill mixes. Many of those skills are just as difficult for the inventor as inventing might be for the non-inventor. In fact, most inventors aren't the most business-minded folks you'll come across.

So focus on your strengths, and surround yourself with people who have strengths in critical areas where you don't. That's how you'll have the best chance of success.

United States Patent [19]

Patterson et al.

[11] **Patent Number:** **5,761,299**

[45] **Date of Patent:** **Jun. 2, 1998**

[54] **AUXILIARY COMPONENT CONNECTOR INCLUDING MICROPHONE CHANNEL**

[75] Inventors: **Gregory S. Patterson**, Morrisville, N.C.; **Wallace G. Keesee**, Rustburg, Va.; **Curtis W. Thornton**, Cary, N.C.

[73] Assignee: **Ericsson Inc.**, Research Triangle Park, N.C.

[21] Appl. No.: **717,803**

[22] Filed: **Sep. 24, 1996**

[51] **Int. Cl.⁶** **H04M 1/00**
[52] **U.S. Cl.** **379/433**; 379/434
[58] **Field of Search** 379/433, 434, 379/428, 429, 399, 436, 420

[56] **References Cited**

U.S. PATENT DOCUMENTS

3,627,930 12/1971 Tolman 379/433

3,969,673 7/1976 Nordlof
4,636,591 1/1987 Kahlus et al 379/433
4,675,903 6/1987 Guletian et al.

FOREIGN PATENT DOCUMENTS

0 663 749 7/1995 European Pat. Off.
195 00 093 8/1995 Germany

Primary Examiner—Jack Chiang
Attorney, Agent, or Firm—Nixon & Vanderhye PC

[57] **ABSTRACT**

A system connector for an electronic device such as a cellular phone is integrally molded with a mic cavity for receiving a device microphone. By incorporating the microphone into the system connector, overall device thickness can be reduced, providing a more efficient use of space than the previous use of separate connectors.

14 Claims, 2 Drawing Sheets

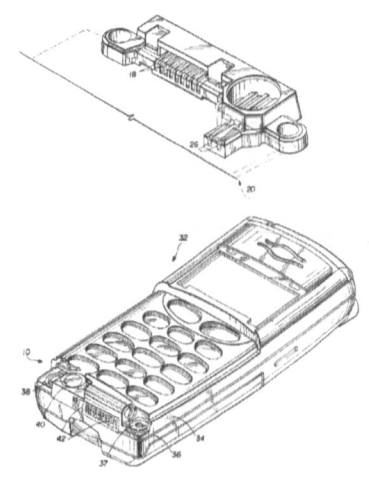

8

Six-Month Rule

We've spent the last several chapters defining some of the attributes most prevalent among inventors. In this chapter, we're going to turn the looking glass around and point out some of the typical weaknesses of the inventor mentality. Why? Because one of the purposes of this book is to help you understand what it takes to develop a business around your ideas and inventions. There's nothing wrong with being an inventor—or perhaps more accurately, a tinkerer—and just enjoying doing those types of things. But building them into a business requires more work and a variety of skills.

There are several areas in which an inventor may have weaknesses. Let's look at what is affectionately known as time to market and what I like to call the six-month rule.

Most people who've been involved with new product development understand time to market. Basically, it's the time it takes to bring a product from concept to the customer. Different products require different development times. You wouldn't expect to bring a commercial jet engine to market in the same time that it takes to get a McDonald's Happy Meal toy into children's eagerly awaiting hands. But within each of those categories, there are smart men and women working hard to develop new products and stay competitive every day.

Inventors aren't typically your most time-conscious individuals. Even simple time-management tasks, like remembering to go into the house for dinner at six, can be elusive. Just imagine how tempting it is for the tinkerer to spend an eternity making incremental improvements.

For that reason, I introduce the six-month rule for your consideration. What is six-month rule? From the time you come up with a novel solution to a problem, resulting in an innovative idea, you have six months before some other smart person in some other town comes up with the same idea—or, at the very least, a competitive solution.

I can't count the number of times I've had what I consider a good idea, only to find with a little searching that there are solutions or products already out there that did the same thing. Where the idea didn't exist already, any procrastination was made evident within a short time as a new product showed up to address the problem.

So, what's the point? If you have a good idea and it isn't already being solved, you can't take a lackadaisical approach at developing it. If you do, and it truly is a problem in need of solution, someone else will solve it. Think of the great inventor duels of the past:

- Tesla (AC power) versus Edison (DC power) for bringing electric power into the home.

- Nikolaus Otto and Alphonse Beau de Roaches for developing the first automobile internal combustion engine (Otto's original patent was overturned in 1886 in favor of the patent granted to de Roaches for his four-stroke engine, though Otto continued to work on the invention while de Roaches's mainly stayed on paper.)

- Even fun things like Leo Fender and Les Paul for developing the solid-body electric guitar.

This isn't a coincidence. If you consider the number of US patents that have been granted in 2011 alone (535,181), it really makes you question why it isn't more often the case.

Furthermore, a lapse in activity can have a detrimental effect on your rights to patent the idea (again, Otto vs. de Roaches), so you can't expect to dream up a cool idea and then let it sit on the shelf to resurrect later. It's fairly well known in the United States that the first to invent something gets credited with the idea. However, people who aren't familiar with the US patenting system may not fully understand how the US Patent and Trademark Office (USPTO) determines the date of invention; the date of invention does not necessarily coincide with the date on which the idea is submitted to the patent office. Rather, the USPTO considers the date on which the inventor actually came up with the idea as the date of invention. In order to prove that an idea was conceived prior to the date on which an individual applied for a patent, that individual must be able to provide evidence that both supports the claimed date of invention and proves that the inventor has been continually improving the idea since its inception

The simplest way to show this continual progress is to document all your work in a journal with pages permanently affixed to the backbone. Date each entry you make, and get a witness to sign and date pages periodically. If you have multiple inventions, have a binder for each invention. Likewise, if you have electronic research or data, print out hard copies, have them signed and dated by a witness, and post them in binders. This sounds somewhat archaic, but if you are diligent, you will end up with a complete history of your invention process, along with witnesses who can corroborate your story. Don't worry if some of the activities lead to dead ends or if you have words crossed out or misspelled. This binder isn't intended to be turned in for an English grade. Those redirects are a part of the invention process and if anything add credence to your invention history in much the same way as showing your work when doing high school algebra.

Unfortunately, the more valuable ideas typically involve areas where there is the greatest market, and the greatest market quite often correlates to a large number of people who face the problem daily. There are a lot of smart men and women facing that problem who are actively pursuing solutions. Don't let your pride get in the way and give you the false impression that you're the only one capable of coming to a solution.

If you don't have the strength or discipline to adhere to time constraints, don't be dismayed. Team up with someone who does. But make sure there's mutual respect. After all, each of you is going to push the other in areas you aren't always comfortable in. If you build the right teams, you will quickly see the value of team synergy.

So, let's recap this chapter. If you have an idea or solution to an existing problem, and there isn't already a viable solution that addresses the problem, you'd better get going, since you probably have a short period before someone else beats you to the punch.

United States Patent [19]

Weadon et al.

[11] Patent Number: 5,700,042

[45] Date of Patent: Dec. 23, 1997

[54] TORSIONALLY-BIASED LATCH ARRANGEMENT

[75] Inventors: **Mark W. Weadon**, Raleigh; **Gregory S. Patterson**, Morrisville, both of N.C.

[73] Assignee: **Ericsson, Inc.**, Research Triangle Park, N.C.

[21] Appl. No.: **685,479**

[22] Filed: **Jul. 24, 1996**

[51] Int. Cl.⁶ E06C 19/06
[52] U.S. Cl. 292/80; 292/87
[58] Field of Search .... 292/80, 87, DIG. 38; 220/324, 326

[56]   **References Cited**

            U.S. PATENT DOCUMENTS

629,523	7/1899	Rarig	292/88
1,491,880	4/1924	Percy	292/87
1,600,497	9/1926	Whellor	292/87
1,744,850	9/1930	Snook	292/89
2,089,371	8/1937	Heller	292/87
3,383,009	5/1968	Weikert	220/324
3,737,067	6/1973	Palson	220/324
3,741,433	6/1973	Bentley et al.	220/326
3,767,110	10/1973	Congleton	220/324
3,846,737	11/1974	Spaulding	220/326

4,212,415	7/1980	Neely	220/324
4,344,646	8/1982	Michel	292/87
4,478,005	10/1984	Mundschenk	292/87
4,501,378	2/1985	Borfield	220/326
4,582,219	4/1986	Mortensen et al.	292/80
4,730,731	3/1988	Allison	292/87
5,285,918	2/1994	Weisburn et al.	220/324
5,427,265	6/1995	Castereds et al.	220/326
5,571,272	11/1996	Roehr et al.	292/80

Primary Examiner—Rodney M. Lindsey
Attorney, Agent, or Firm—Jenkens & Gilchrist, P.C.

[57]   **ABSTRACT**

A cover for a housing is maintained in a fixed position with respect to the housing by a latch arrangement that has at least one edge surface disposed along one edge of a flange which engages a mating surface on the housing when the cover is assembled with the housing. The other side of the flange is integrally formed with an elongated beam that is attached to the cover structure. The elongated beam is torsionally loaded upon assembly of the cover with the housing, and provides a bias force on the edge surface of the flange to maintain the forcible engagement of the edge surface with a mating surface of the housing. The latch arrangement combines the cost effectiveness and space efficiency characteristics of plastic latch designs with the durability, dependability and tactile qualities of mechanical spring arrangements.

17 Claims, 2 Drawing Sheets

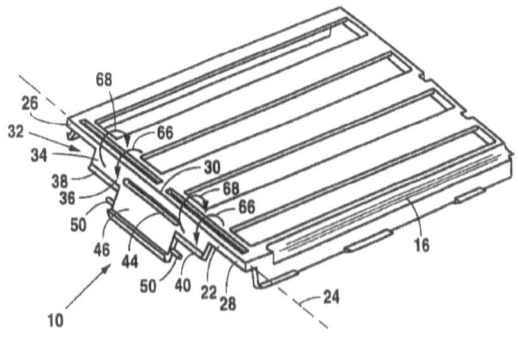

9

Look Again

So you have a great idea. Now you're ready to patent your idea to protect your future fortune—or maybe just to start making the product. Humans have been wandering around the face of the earth for a long time now, improving their world all the way. So the chances of you truly being the first and only one to come up with a unique idea are pretty slim. If you want to avoid future heartache, or worse yet, investing money into something only to discover the idea already exists, you need to search exhaustively—and then look again.

Before I decide to spend money on a patent attorney, I go to the United States Patent and Trademark Organization (www.uspto.gov) to make sure there is nothing out there that obviously looks like my idea. This is a free link where you can search from nearly the entire list of granted patents. Just click on the Search button under the Patent heading in the left column. The site has online help to answer most of your search questions, but it's simple once you get used to it. However, you must have patience. Depending on the topic, you can expect multiple patents to review.

For example, even a quick search on the term "solar cell" yields 13,899 patents.

Like any search, there are numbers of keywords and search methods that you can and should utilize. Take your time and try them all. Look at the patents that come up as hits, and print off or note the ones that seem closest to your idea. Also look at patents that were cited as "prior art" in these disclosures, and look in detail at those. Basically, what you'll end up with is a long thread of patents that cited earlier patents, and so on. I'll say it again: the chance of typing in a keyword and not getting any hits is very low. If it does happen, you probably didn't do a good job of picking a relevant keyword. Don't believe me? Consider this eclectic list of search topics that returned hits:

- Sushi knife: 2 patents, including No. 5,872,813, "Device for Making Rolled Sushi"

- Baby doll: 119 patents, including No. D560,732, "Biblical Baby Doll"

- Dog bath: 7 patents including. No. 5,213,064, "Animal Bath Apparatus having Multiple Spray Assemblies"

- Whoopee cushion: 3 patents, including No. 6,241,620, "Simulated Shattered Glass Novelty Device with Method of Use"

And these are just the main search returns. Each of these patents cites multiple prior patents of a similar nature that should also be reviewed.

This process can take many hours, even days, but the information will be invaluable as you determine the breadth of claims your idea has. Plus, it's good data to take to your patent attorney when the time comes to get him or her involved.

The next thing you should do is an Internet search—using a free search engine, like Google or Yahoo—to look for "prior art." Without getting into the full legal meaning of that term, we can sum it up by saying that if you find a public record of an idea close to your next great invention, this previous public disclosure of the idea can prevent you from making patent claims or severely narrow the claims you can make on your idea. The advent of the Internet age has definitely made this a much simpler task, but it's still one of those tasks that folks don't seem to want to do. It's a lot more fun to work through the details of your invention than to spend time in front of the computer, searching what will seem like an endless number of Google hits.

In this broader prior art search, look for written documentation or for products already on the market. Once the idea becomes public knowledge, either by publishing a description of the idea or by selling a product embodying the idea, the USPTO prevents all others from patenting that idea as their own, regardless of whether or not the idea was previously patented.

Another good source is to go to company or university sites that focus on the area you're inventing in. This is especially true if your idea isn't a product as much as it is a component in a product or software. Searching these sites will give you a good understanding of what's out there and where to look next.

Finally, search design company sites (such as www. porticos.net), and look at their portfolio sections. These companies often develop products for a wide range of customers—some big clients that you would have heard of and some small clients that you might not have heard of. Since their portfolio sections are often a key source of marketing, they're typically eager to show their list of accomplishments so you can see what they've done before. Again, consider the threads that these may lead to. For example, you might see a product that isn't exactly like what you were thinking, but it might give you another company name to search by to see if they have other products that more closely apply to your idea.

All the work you have put into a preliminary prior art search, doesn't negate the need for a true prior art search made by a reputable patent attorney. I'm not talking about one that runs infomercial ads that saying that for $59.99 you will get a packet that has all you need to know to get rich off your idea. I mean a real patent attorney who is familiar with the specific area of expertise of your idea. While you can file your own patent claim, keep in mind that the patent process can be a long and complicated one. For example, at the time of this writing, the patent office charge for filing a utility patent (including filing, examination, and allowance fees) ranges from 2,400 to 3,000 dollars, depending on whether you have a separate search done or not.

It has been my personal experience that it takes two to three years from the time you submit the patent application until you get a formal response, and 90 percent of the time, that response is a rejection due to a problem with a claim. You then have to address the rejection issue and resubmit. In all, you can expect three to four years to get the application approved.

The quality with which your application is done goes a long way in determining its success and the eventual patent value. That's why I recommend working with a patent attorney; there are only so many hours in a day, so focus on your strengths, and let others do the same. If you truly believe you have a novel and valuable idea, you'll be doing yourself a huge favor by paying someone with the right experience to help you protect it properly.

These two simple steps—Look (search the USPTO site) and Look Again (do Internet searches)—can save you much heartache. I think you'll be amazed at the near misses that you'll encounter during your searches. Look at them objectively or have a colleague look at them, then proceed accordingly.

US006195839B1

(12) **United States Patent**
Patterson et al.

(10) Patent No.: **US 6,195,839 B1**
(45) Date of Patent: **Mar. 6, 2001**

(54) HINGED DETENT

(75) Inventors: Gregory S. Patterson, Morrisville; Thomas D. Snyder, Raleigh, both of NC (US)

(73) Assignee: Ericsson Inc., Research Triangle Park, NC (US)

(*) Notice: Subject to any disclaimer, the term of this patent is extended or adjusted under 35 U.S.C. 154(b) by 0 days.

(21) Appl. No.: 08/926,146

(22) Filed: Sep. 9, 1997

(51) Int. Cl.⁷ B41J 50/10
(52) U.S. Cl. 16/334; 16/326; 16/329; 400/682; 400/489
(58) Field of Search 16/328, 329, 331, 16/332, 334; 361/680; 400/682, 489, 472

(56) References Cited

U.S. PATENT DOCUMENTS

1,031,287	*	7/1912	Page 16/332
1,180,669	*	4/1916	Oehlrich et al. 16/334
2,635,281		4/1953	Feldberg 16/341
3,561,387	*	2/1971	Lawrence, Jr. 16/121
3,990,565	*	11/1976	Felton et al. .... 400/489 X
4,980,829	*	4/1986	Metheopoulos 16/334
5,022,118	*	6/1991	Woo Li 16/334
5,073,050	*	12/1991	Andrews .... 400/489 X
5,267,127	*	11/1993	Pollit 361/680
5,318,307	*	6/1994	Braun et al. .... 400/489 X
5,412,842	*	5/1995	Riblett 16/334
5,465,925	*	11/1995	Galvey .... 400/489 X
5,537,013	*	4/1996	Weedon et al. 16/334
5,574,481	*	11/1996	Lee .... 400/489 X
5,596,486	*	1/1997	Munsee et al. 361/680
5,612,861	*	3/1997	Mutimum .... 400/489 X
5,615,081	*	3/1997	Ma 361/680
5,651,622	*	7/1997	Kim 400/480
5,659,307	*	8/1997	Karidis et al. .... 400/480 X
5,734,548	*	3/1998	Park 361/680
5,769,551	*	6/1998	Isai et al. 400/480
5,841,633	*	11/1998	Sadler et al. 361/740

FOREIGN PATENT DOCUMENTS

726,39,81	1/1982	(AU) .	
1 006 356 B	1/1957	(DE) .	
42 39 398 A1	5/1991	(DE) .	
61519	* 11/1983	(DK)	16/331
0 640 489 A2	3/1995	(EP) .	
0 782 474 A1	9/1996	(EP) .	
0 772 333 A2	5/1997	(EP) .	
0 777 369 A2	6/1997	(EP) .	
100273	3/1998	(EP) .	
1293349	* 11/1960	(FR)	16/334
2089301	1/1972	(FR) .	
2 629 510 A1	10/1989	(FR) .	
404854	* 1/1934	(GB)	16/332
1560723	* 2/1980	(GB)	16/334
2 300 860	11/1996	(GB) .	
2 303 427	2/1997	(GB) .	
107730	* 6/1943	(SE)	16/334
WO 90/13728	2/1990	(WO) .	

* cited by examiner

Primary Examiner—Anthony Knight
(74) Attorney, Agent, or Firm—Jenkens & Gilchrist, P.C.

(57) **ABSTRACT**

Two pivoting portions of a product are connected by a hinged detent. The hinged detent provides a snap feel when the product halves are closed or opened to an operable angle. It also allows for the placement of wires and connectors within the hinge. The hinged detent design further enables easy vertical axis assembly and provides for one of a multiple of operable angles to be factory-set. In adjustable hinge detents, a dial or similar mechanism can be rotated to adjust and set the desired operable angle to which the hinged product halves will be opened. Locating elements are forcibly disengaged from one set of adjusting recesses in the adjustable hinge, then rotated to different adjusting recesses of the hinge, and finally permitted to reengage the adjustable hinge in the new adjusting recesses. This mechanism permits a multitude of operable angles to be selected. Each time the product portions are reopened, they will automatically open to the previously selected angle. The adjustable hinge detent can be used, for example, to connect two v-keyboard halves, a screen to a laptop base, two components of collapsing headphones, or two parts of an adjustable stand.

32 Claims, 23 Drawing Sheets

10

Marketing Is King

If questioned, most inventors would say the most importance aspect of an invention is its design. And that's what I think of when I think of the word *invention*. But that's only part of the puzzle. If your sole reason for inventing is to try to get more patents associated with your name than Thomas Edison (good luck), you must be attuned to the market, both in terms of what the market wants and how to market the invention. Let's talk about *marketing* first.

I'm sure that more than a few of my readers either have a Pocket Fisherman in the closet or gave one to their dad for Father's Day. If you don't know, the Pocket Fisherman is a portable fishing rod that includes storage for your lures and folds into a compact, easy-to-carry shape. You can still find them in numerous big department stores or on the Internet.

Now, can you name the inventor? You may not know with confidence who invented it, but I bet you can name the marketing guy who used to do the infomercials, Mr. Ron Popeil. If you aren't familiar with his name, please pretend that you are for the sake of this story. (It was a trick question anyway, since Ron's father invented the Pocket Fisherman originally, then Ron "reinvented" it some time later.)

The point is that the Pocket Fisherman (or the Veg-O-Matic or Chop-O-Matic or . . .) probably wouldn't be considered a particularly technical patent. I mean, you don't picture a room full of scientists hovering around a Petri dish when you think of the Pocket Fisherman. However, because of incredible marketing, Ronco sold many millions of those types of devices over the years and laughed all the way to the bank. Although many such products made their debut in the early to mid-1960s in late-night infomercials, "As Seen on TV" spots, and various other locations, they're still being sold today. For $19.99, you can get your very own Veg-O-Matic from Amazon.

So, if I consider this along with the fact that Mr. Popeil has numerous patents like it to his name, I'd say he's not only an inventor, but a financially successful one at that.

According to the American Marketing Association (AMA), "marketing is the process of planning and executing the conception, pricing, promotion, and distribution of ideas, goods, and services to create exchanges that satisfy individual and organizational objectives." Whether this is the definition you had in mind or not, it's easy to see that for an idea to become successful (either financially or as a humanitarian solution), you must put a lot of effort and thought into how to market it to the potential customer. Failure to do so means that your idea, however wonderful, will probably be destined for the dusty patent archives somewhere. Its only hope for resurfacing will be as a prior art reference on some future patent. Regardless of who does the marketing (you or a firm you might hire), successful marketing requires a good understanding of the *market*.

When considering the market, the law of economics trumps the law of physics. If you have a solution but really no problem that needs to be solved, you really don't have much. You might not consider yourself a salesperson, but if you've developed an idea, you probably have more knowledge of the market than you might suspect. What were the things that made you come up with your new idea? Who are the types of people who would have similar problems as you did when your new idea spawned?

Follow the thread from there until you're fully versed in the market that your idea is suited for. Learn all you can about the type of people who might be interested in the product. If it's not a consumer-related idea or product, that doesn't let you off the hook. Perhaps the right customers to consider are university or science organizations. In today's Internet world, everyone with a computer can get a respectable amount of information on the market just by searching.

I can tell you from experience that even if you do hire a marketing firm, one of the first things they're going to do is ask you about the market. Sure, they'll have access to detailed tools for identifying volumes of similar products and other things, but in the beginning, they need to learn what your idea is and what market you think is most applicable.

The more you know about the market, the more effective your marketing campaign will be. And it will allow you to do a better job of deciding if the idea has financial merit or not.

There is a variety of ways to understand the market, but typically I do an Internet search and follow the thread. For example:

1) First, I search for similar products on the market.

2) Then I look at who manufactured those products, searching those manufacturing sites down to subsuppliers, as applicable.

3) Going the other way, I search deeper into the companies that sell the product and ultimately down to the type of customer that uses the product. Perhaps there's a product group right in your back yard that you can sit down with and talk to, or a trade show that's coming to town that you can attend to learn more about the field.

4) I do searches in various publications that record sales volumes, revenues, and other data from all the companies identified (the distributor, the customer group, and the manufacturing sources). This gives me an idea of cost margins and sales volumes. Almost every product group has some association that tracks progress and trends. Sometime you need to purchase the information. Sometimes it's free.

5) I also search for blogs or other articles that rate products that are similar to my idea. You can get a good feel for what the competition is doing well and what things should be done better. Then you can ask yourself, *How does this line up with the improvements I feel my product makes over the competition's product?*

When you have the data, be honest with yourself and true to the data. Don't try to put a square peg in a round hole. You'll end up frustrated, and the peg still won't fit.

Once you understand the market and you understand what position you want to play in the market, you can start to formulate a solid marketing plan that will address your goal. Perhaps you want to manufacture, or you want to license the idea to someone else to manufacture, or you just want to sell the entire idea outright. If marketing isn't your strength, consider teaming up with someone or a company that does have this strength. But be aware that marketing can be a very costly proposition, so before you get in too deep, be sure to understand the costs and what you will be getting for those costs. Compare this cost with the market knowledge you gained previously (product cost pressures, volumes, etc.) to come to a decision on whether this expense can be supported by the potential sales. If not, the answer isn't to skip the marketing; the answer is likely that the idea isn't going to return financial rewards worth pursuing.

Even though we've only scratched the surface, you can see that understanding the market and the marketing of the idea (or product) are critical aspects of getting a return on your brainchild. So you need to tackle them with the same gusto and detail that you do when you're sitting at the CAD station and modeling up that next great idea.

US006038742A

United States Patent [19]

Patterson

[11] Patent Number: 6,038,742

[45] Date of Patent: Mar. 21, 2000

[54] **SWIVEL CLIP FOR RELEASABLY SECURING PERSONAL ARTICLES**

[75] Inventor: **Gregory S. Patterson**, Morrisville, N.C.

[73] Assignee: **Ericsson Inc.**, Research Triangle Park, N.C.

[21] Appl. No.: **09/253,461**

[22] Filed: **Feb. 22, 1999**

[51] Int. Cl.[7] **A44B 21/00**; A45F 5/00
[52] U.S. Cl. **24/3.12**; 24/3.11; 24/597; 24/665; 24/669
[58] Field of Search 24/3.12, 3.11, 24/575, 597, 665, 669; 224/197

[56] **References Cited**

U.S. PATENT DOCUMENTS

2,326,558	8/1943	Pelz	24/3.11
3,984,191	10/1976	Doty	24/669
4,419,794	12/1983	Horton, Jr. et al.	24/669

5,347,693	9/1994	Otrusina	24/3.12
5,622,296	4/1997	Pirhonen et al.	
5,839,173	11/1998	Otrusina	24/597

FOREIGN PATENT DOCUMENTS

0135878	6/1948	Australia	24/665
0818988	8/1959	United Kingdom	24/665

Primary Examiner—Victor N. Sakran
Attorney, Agent, or Firm—Woods, Phillips, VanSanten, Clark & Mortimer

[57] **ABSTRACT**

A clip is provided for releasably securing an article of personal use, the article having a stud with a head spaced from the article. The clip includes a base connectable to a strap and a spring member biased against the base. The base includes a recess hole adapted to receive the stud head. The spring member includes a slot therein extending to an end substantially aligned with the recess hole, with the aligned end of the slot having a first width less than a diameter of the stud head.

24 Claims, 3 Drawing Sheets

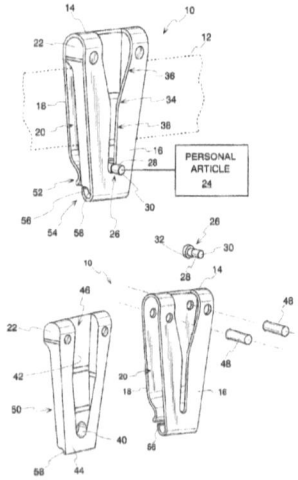

11

Evolutionary Versus Revolutionary

Evolution and revolution are interesting criteria by which many inventors critique their ideas, whether they mean to or not. Then they discard evolutionary ideas as having little value in the grand scheme of things.

I confess that I've never had what I would consider a revolutionary idea. This tends to disappoint me from time to time. But in doing some research for this section, I see that perhaps my standards are too high.

More importantly, with regard to the topic of making money from your ideas or patents, does success rely only on revolutionary ideas? Can they be the only way of getting the proverbial "pot of gold" at the end of the invention rainbow?

When I consider the definitions of *evolutionary* or *revolutionary*, I would say that they are consistent to my basic philosophy. *Evolution*, according to an

Internet dictionary, is a process in which something passes by degrees to a different stage. Hence, the Theory of Evolution, where supposedly man has evolved over eons from lesser organisms that have struggled to adapt to changing conditions. Compare that to *revolution*, a drastic and far-reaching change.

What comes to your mind when you think of revolutionary ideas?: the theory of relativity by Albert Einstein, the theory of gravity by Sir Isaac Newton, or the reported hidden secrets in Leonardo Da Vinci's paintings? Perhaps that's just from a movie; I can never keep it straight. How about the Wright brothers and powered, human-controlled flight? All of these are examples of revolutionary thinkers whose their ideas revolutionized some aspect of civilized life. But were the ideas themselves revolutionary or evolutionary?

Let's consider air travel, since everyone is probably impacted by—and it's pretty darn cool too. There are still many folks around who were alive when jet engines were nothing more than curiosities, burping and farting hot gases in the lab. Interestingly, that picture reminds me of someone I know, but I'll keep to the subject. Frank Whittle, who applied for a patent on his jet engine in 1930, and Hans Von Ohain, who was working independently and in parallel (another fine example of why it's good to follow the six-month rule) and whose engine is credited with supporting the first jet plane flight in 1935, might both be considered as having a revolutionary idea.

But I believe that these and any other ideas I've seen or read about over history were really evolutionary, not revolutionary. In this example, centrifugal compressors, which were at the heart of the early jet engines, were already in use as superchargers on piston engines. Deriving power from the expansion associated with combustion or super-heated gases was not new. Again, the piston engine was doing that, and before gas pistons was the steam engine. Steam engines evolved over time from the 1712 Atmospheric Engine of Thomas Newcomen to the high-pressure "Cornish" engine of Olivar Evans and Richard Trevithick.

But even this was preceded by other inventors, all the way down to King Heron from first-century Egypt, who's Aelopile (essentially a steam-driven jet engine) was opening temple doors. It reminds me of the Old Testament; Heron begat so and so, who begat so and so, until the present day.

I'm not arguing that any of these examples—from the steam engines role in the Industrial Revolution to the jet engine's role in the historic rise of manned flight—did not cause a drastic and far-reaching change in the ways of thinking and behavior (that is the definition of revolutionary). But the process by which these ideas were developed was very evolutionary indeed.

Though Newton or da Vinci may not have had throngs of text or research from previous inventors to guide them as they developed their theories on gravity or flight, but they had nature all around them. Couple that with an innate curiosity and strong powers of observation, and you have the bases for their ideas.

Unless you were born in a cave and never allowed contact with the outside world (I think another famous person discussed this at one time), your ideas are bound to be impacted or somehow guided by what you see around you and the experiences you've had. So don't discount your evolutionary ideas as unimportant. Who knows when one of those might be the next to revolutionize our world?

(12) **United States Patent**
Sadler et al.

(10) Patent No.: **US 6,238,230 B1**
(45) Date of Patent: **May 29, 2001**

(54) **LATCH ASSEMBLY AND CONNECTOR ASSEMBLY INCLUDING THE SAME**

(75) Inventors: **John T. Sadler**, Wake Forest; **Gregory S. Patterson**, Morrisville, both of NC (US)

(73) Assignee: **Telefonaktiebolaget L.M. Ericsson** (SE)

(*) Notice: Subject to any disclaimer, the term of this patent is extended or adjusted under 35 U.S.C. 154(b) by 0 days.

(21) Appl. No.: **09/639,222**

(22) Filed: **Aug. 15, 2000**

(51) Int. Cl.⁷ **H01R 13/627**

(52) U.S. Cl. **439/350**; 439/357

(58) Field of Search 439/350, 352, 439/353, 354, 357, 567

(56) **References Cited**

U.S. PATENT DOCUMENTS

3,964,364	* 6/1976	Poe	85/72
4,630,983	* 12/1986	Fischer	411/15
4,830,556	* 5/1989	Nelson	411/41
4,861,208	* 8/1989	Boundy	411/339
5,848,456	* 12/1998	Sjoqvist	24/618

* cited by examiner

Primary Examiner—Tulsidas Patel
(74) *Attorney, Agent, or Firm*—Myers Bigel Sibley & Sajovec

(57) **ABSTRACT**

A latch assembly includes a body member defining a cavity and including at least two spaced apart, opposed, relatively displaceable arms. A latch structure is located on at least one of the arms. A deformable elastomeric core is disposed in the cavity to resist convergent displacement of the arms. The elastomeric core is responsive to convergent displacement of the arms to provide a spring force biasing the arms apart.

29 Claims, 4 Drawing Sheets

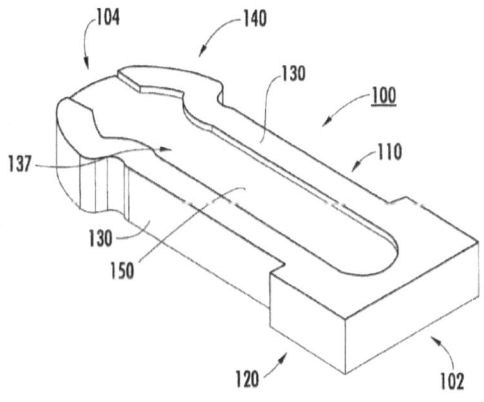

12

All or Nothing

It should be obvious by now that taking an idea from concept to reality is a tough assignment. In this chapter, we'll discuss the shortfalls with trying to make that transition successfully as a part-time activity.

As we've discussed before, many inventors are tinkerers at heart. They work normal jobs forty hours a week and spend their weekend in the shop, developing the next great invention. I think this is a great use of time. It exercises the creative side of your brain and build on your strengths and interests. For the most part, the investment in material is probably less than you would have spent on other frivolous activities, given that much free time on your hands. Who knows? It's like the lottery; perhaps you might just come up with an invention that works.

However, if you do plan to build a business, you can't rely on lottery odds. You need a solid plan that yields a solid return on your investment—a plan that accounts for the resources required to develop not only the initial idea, but also the complementary products that must follow shortly after.

Still don't think it's a full-time job? Consider the amount of time you already have in conceptualizing and prototyping the idea. Now add time to patent, time to market, time to manage resources, even the time just to put together the plan in the first place. It's more than a full-time job; it's a full-time job for several people. Anything less isn't a road toward building a successful business. It's just an interesting hobby.

To build a business, you must be completely devoted to the endeavor. I'm not advocating ditching your current forty-hour-a-week-job with the intention of dreaming up profitable ideas. There can (and probably should) be some transition associated with your plan.

Let's assume that you already have an idea or solid kernel that serves as the cornerstone and that you have considered some of the other topics that we discussed over the last many pages. The successful business plan will have some transition from the part-time tinkering stage to full-time development and production.

This is a good time to point out that there are non-profit agencies available to help you create your business plan. For example, here in North Carolina, you can go to the CED (www.cednc.org) to get mentoring and support on everything from putting together your business plan to identifying investment opportunities. Check with local and state small-business agencies to see what options exist for you.

If your current financial situation (or your own intestinal fortitude) isn't conducive to making the transition cleanly, consider some alternate plans. At Porticos, we chose to base the business initially on service-oriented revenue while we develop ideas that we could transition into a stand-alone business. Why? We were not financially capable of going years without personal income while an idea was developed, marketed, and brought into production. Conversely, we could develop the service side of the business more easily, providing a recurring revenue stream and keeping our engineering talents current.

As a result, we are on the brink of realizing fruit from our labor. We created a separate company called Porticool to finish the development and marketing of the cooling vest product that we patented, and we have successfully negotiated a licensing agreement.

In keeping with the advice I'm giving you, we are transitioning now from part-time resources that have supported that project to full-time resources tasked not only with industrialization of that original idea but also with successfully running the business and developing the follow-on or complementary ideas. These tasks are crucial to building a profitable business.

Now that Porticool is responsible for its own profit and loss, Porticos can continue to focus on the service side and on developing new ideas for different markets. Ultimately, one of those new ideas will spawn into another stand-alone company, and so on.

In summary, developing a business around your inventions is in many ways no different from building any other long-term profitable company. It can't be maintained on a part-time basis, but rather requires planning and dedicated support to become successful. Anything less is really just a hobby.

That doesn't mean you should give up inventing altogether. As I noted in the introduction, if you have the inventing spirit, you almost have no choice but to keep dreaming up and developing your ideas, at least at some level. There are still opportunities for you to generate revenue from those ideas, but most likely it would be through a licensing agreement or something similar, as I will discuss in the next chapter. The sooner you come to terms with your situation in light of that argument, the easier it will be to know how to proceed and the better you will sleep at night.

13

Extraction

In this book, I use the word *extraction* to define the process by which the inventor derives income from an idea. We've spent a lot of time focusing on the invention process itself. We've considered important aspects, ranging from how to perform a patent search to how you can effectively allocate activities to best utilize your skill set. Ultimately, the hope is that there will be a pot of gold at the end of the invention rainbow.

Making money is not a criterion for being an inventor. You could just be doing this for a hobby or perhaps for academic reasons. But if you intend to make this a business, getting paid is a necessity. So what are some options for extraction?

Probably the simplest option (and the most desirable from the individual or part-time inventor's standpoint) is to license the idea or technology to a company that already focuses on the product area or is interested in expanding into that field. This approach presents many advantages to the inventor.

Here are few of the more important ones:

1) The financial investment required by the inventor is reduced greatly, because he or she doesn't need to support industrialization and production expenses. He or she can avoid tooling, materials, marketing, sales, and customer support costs, which are significant.

2) The liability associated with the sale and use of the product is diminished. That's not to say that the inventor is completely protected. Lawyers look for as many targets as possible, so fundamental design-related negligence will probably find its way back to you. However, higher-risk items like manufacturing quality, user awareness, and consumer risk are more often the responsibility of the manufacturer or sales company.

3) The sales and marketing channels are already in place and supported by the licensing company. Developing these channels yourself can be a costly and time-consuming adventure, to say the least. In many cases, there will be competition in the market already that will probably better funded and firmly entrenched, which makes entering those markets by yourself very difficult.

Of course, there are downsides to licensing your technology as well. The most obvious is a reduction in the potential profit. That makes sense; greater risk needs to yield greater reward to make it worth doing at all. By acknowledging that a straight license agreement has less risk for the inventor, we must acknowledge that the reward would be reduced accordingly. This is not to say that reward can't be very handsome, but licensees wouldn't be buying ideas if they didn't believe they could make many more times return on their investment. I also don't want to give the impression that licensing is an easy, slam-dunk approach to generating revenue from your ideas. You will still have to put a lot of effort into finding potential licensees and doing the things it takes to get them excited about your invention. Later in this chapter, I'll discuss methods for finding potential investors.

As I've stated before regarding a good patent attorney, you really need to consider the services of a reputable attorney to draft and support any license agreement. You and your prospective licensee can *and should* agree, in layman's terms, to what you expect from each other. Yet an expert is needed to formulate a fair and legal written contract between the two parties. The cost for this activity will vary with the complexity of the agreements, so simpler is always better. At a minimum, you will need to consider ten to twenty hours of an attorney at 250 dollars per hour.

At the other end of the spectrum, the inventor may decide to industrialize the technology into a product and then sell to distributors, through sales representatives or directly to customers. Compared to the straight license agreement, this scenario can yield higher rewards, but the risks and costs are greater as well.

My experience has shown that a number of factors determine the path you take. Obvious factors are your financial backing and risk aversion. One of the less obvious factors is *prototype difficulty*. How easy is it to prototype or otherwise demonstrate the technology so that it can be envisioned as a final product? Not everyone can extrapolate from back-of-the-napkin sketches to a final product. The shorter the distance the potential licensee has to extrapolate, the more likely a license agreement can be reached.

It's worth restating: no company that manufactures or sells products is going to shell out money for a license agreement unless it feels that the return on investment will be worth it. The only way they will know that is if they have a complete grasp of the technology. You must show the potential licensee how the benefits of your technology will result in greater sales. The licensee must see the path to industrialize the technology and thereby make money.

For this reason, many ideas aren't conducive to a simple technology license agreement. So the inventor must pursue industrializing the product, with hope to either sell the product or plan to sell the company after the value to the market is established.

How do you find a potential licensee? The work you did in developing your idea can help you generate a list of potential licensees. Manufacturers, distributors, and turnkey corporations involved with similar products or customers are good leads, but be careful how you approach these entities. Make sure solid nondisclosure agreements are in place and, whenever possible, present any material or prototypes in person. Keep a record of who you presented to and when. You want to show enough to generate excitement and facilitate discussions, but you never want to teach the prospective licensee how to replicate or, worse yet, circumvent your idea.

Another good strategy is to visit trade shows or conferences in your specific field of interest. This, coupled with a list of potential companies, can lay the groundwork for face-to-face discussions. Another advantage of trade shows is that you will see and be seen by others who might not have shown up in your earlier searches. Be prepared for a lot of cold shoulders and closed doors. What you are doing is akin to the telemarketing calls you try to avoid at home.

Regardless of the approach you choose, don't plan on it being simple or quick. You will need patience and perseverance to get to the point where you can expect a return on your ideas.

This is a good time to remind you to be realistic with your skills. If you aren't well suited for sales activities, partner with someone who is. You also need to be realistic with the value of the idea and be ready to negotiate. While we hope that all our hard work and research improves our odds of success, some good ideas never get to the point of extracting revenue. Recall from our first chapter that only one in a thousand ideas brings value to the inventor. Yes, you need to maintain your passion, but know when to pull the plug and move on.

Extracting revenue from an invention is really where the rubber meets the road. In many ways, it's the defining line between inventing as a hobby and building a business.

US007527612B1

(12) **United States Patent**
    Carpenter et al.

(10) Patent No.: **US 7,527,612 B1**
(45) **Date of Patent:** **May 5, 2009**

(54) **COOLING DEVICE**

(75) Inventors: **William K. Carpenter**, Durham, NC
(US); **Gregory S. Patterson**,
Morrisville, NC (US); **Sean M. Ahr**,
Morrisville, NC (US); **Jonathan Deline**,
Morrisville, NC (US); **Debbie Deline**,
Morrisville, NC (US)

(73) Assignee: **Porticool, Inc.**, Morrisville, NC (US)

(*) Notice: Subject to any disclaimer, the term of this
patent is extended or adjusted under 35
U.S.C. 154(b) by 434 days.

(21) Appl. No.: **11/142,637**

(22) Filed: **Jun. 1, 2005**

Related U.S. Application Data

(60) Provisional application No. 60/587,756, filed on Jul.
14, 2004.

(51) **Int. Cl.**
     A61F 7/00   (2006.01)
(52) **U.S. Cl.** **604/291**; 62/269.3
(58) **Field of Classification Search** 604/291–293;
     607/107, 96, 108 111; 165/46; 62/259.3
     See application file for complete search history.

(56) **References Cited**

U.S. PATENT DOCUMENTS

3,049,896 A * 8/1962 Webb 128/201.25

4,738,119 A *	4/1988	Zafred	607/104
5,438,707 A *	8/1995	Horn	2/457
6,209,144 B1 *	4/2001	Carter	2/458
6,295,648 B2 *	10/2001	Siman-Tov et al.	2/2.5
6,584,798 B2 *	7/2003	Schegerin	62/386
6,681,589 B2 *	1/2004	Brudnicki	62/259.3

FOREIGN PATENT DOCUMENTS

GB   1376604 A * 12/1974

* cited by examiner

Primary Examiner—Tatyana Zalukaeva
Assistant Examiner—Lynne Anderson
(74) *Attorney, Agent, or Firm*—Coats & Bennett, P.L.L.C.

(57)   **ABSTRACT**

A cooling garment including an inlet for receiving a cooling
medium such as CO_2. A series of conduits are associated with
the garment. In a first cooling stage, the cooling medium or
CO_2 passes through the one or more conduits and undergoes
a phase change where the cooling medium or CO_2 changes
from a predominantly liquid phase to a predominantly gaseous phase. In this first stage, heat is transferred from a living
body having the garment disposed adjacent thereto the cooling medium or CO_2. In a second stage of cooling, the cooling
medium or CO_2 assumes a substantial gaseous phase and the
gaseous cooling medium or CO_2 is dispersed onto the garment or the body resulting in the body being cooled through
evaporative cooling.

15 Claims, 4 Drawing Sheets

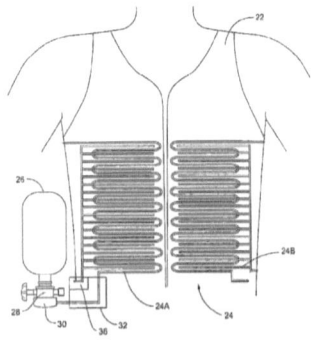

14

Final Words

It seems like a long journey since we started investigating what it takes to patent an idea or extract revenue from your inventions. I hope the information presented has been helpful or at the very least made for entertaining reading.

Let's review the main points that we've discussed:

- *Risk versus reward.* It's often been said that there are no rewards without taking risks. But what people fail to consider when evaluating ideas for development is how much risk they are capable of taking—and not strictly monetarily. Risks include availability of time and advancements in technology as well as liability risks that will be attached to the final product.

- *By the numbers.* When it's all said and done, successful ideas need to be backed up by the numbers. We reviewed the financial fundamentals to developing a business from your inventions.

- *The single-product myth.* One product does not constitute a viable long-term business. You need a portfolio to run a business. Likewise, if you're interested more in part-time inventing as a hobby with potential upsides, then the more ideas you generate, the greater the odds that one will be of interest.

- *Passion.* Developing and driving an idea from concept to the market isn't for the faint of heart. Innovation has to be a passion. The kernel must excite the inventor, or it isn't going to stand the rigors of development.

- *Six-month rule.* You can't pursue ideas in a lackluster way, because you'll be beat to the market. There are many smart people looking for similar solutions, so time is a factor if you want to reap the rewards.

- *Look again.* Humans have been wandering around on the face of the earth a long time now. The chance of you truly being the first and only one to come up with a particular idea is slim. If you want to avoid heartache or, worse yet, investing money in something, only to discover the idea already exists, you need to search exhaustively, and then look again.

- *Market is king.* Understanding the market and the marketing of the idea (or product) are critical aspects of getting a return on your investment. If you develop a product with no market in mind, you run the risk of finding a solution where there isn't a problem.

- *Evolution versus revolution.* We discussed the differences between evolutionary and revolutionary ideas, making the point that both are valuable to the invention process.

- *All or nothing.* Taking an idea from concept to reality is a tough assignment. Add to that the time constraints and associated pressures, and it is apparent that developing a business around your ideas can't be viewed as a part-time endeavor. If you don't have a plan to transition to a full-time effort, focus on invention more as a hobby with the potential to license an idea if you come up with something of real commercial value.

- *Extraction.* If you're going to invent with the intention to make money, you need to consider how you plan to extract value from the invention when developing and investing in an idea. Your extraction plans should and will affect design and marketing plans.

With all the potential pitfalls, trials, and tribulations associated with inventing and product design, you might be tempted to ask the question that we posed in the introduction chapter: "Why do it at all?" For what it's worth, let me give you my response.

First and foremost, I enjoy coming up with ideas and solutions to problems that no one has solved before. Consider it slightly egotistical, but it's exciting when you get that "aha" moment and the idea starts to develop right in front of your eyes. Inventors can develop a legacy. Thomas Edison, Nikolai Tesla, and Albert Einstein are long gone, but their names live on through the many inventions they contributed to society—inventions still relevant now.

Second, I believe a major driver of inventing is the creative outlet that you get. Regardless of whether you're a factory worker or a CEO, you have the opportunity to come up with a novel idea. In the same way that artists express their creativity on canvas for others to enjoy, inventors manipulate past ideas, personal knowledge, and life experiences to create a new form of art—one conveyed through words, formulas, and hardware.

Third is the prospect of financial reward. Granted, you could argue that the lottery might have better odds, but inventing and developing products from those inventions has less to do with chance and more to do with skill. Royalties and/or sale of intellectual property (IP) have the advantage of reaping financial gain not tied directly to the inventor's available working hours. To say it another way, engineers can make a good, solid living by providing engineering support, but they are limited by the sheer number of hours they can work. Conversely, revenue from IP or products spawned from the IP are tied to market factors and not the inventor's availability.

And finally, ask yourself, *What else would I be doing with my time?* There are only so many hours of TV or rounds of golf that you can stand (or afford). Inventing can be a great escape; you can look at it as a hobby that can reap financial or personal rewards. It doesn't suffer from any of the traditional boundaries of age, race, or gender. People from all walks of life have inventions.

So while I still maintain that points we have discussed in this book are valuable to anyone wanting to start a business that extracts revenue from his or her inventions, I readily admit that there are intangible benefits to the inventor that can't and should not be underestimated.

So go forth and invent something new!